Clara Barton

and the American Red Cross

by Eve Marko

illustrations by Pablo Marcos

ABDO
Publishing Company

HEROES OF AMERICA™

Edited by
Joshua E. Hanft and Rochelle Larkin

visit us at
www.abdopub.com

Library edition published in 2005 by ABDO Publishing Company, 4940 Viking Drive, Suite 622, Edina, Minnesota 55435. Published by agreement with Playmore Incorporated Publishers and Waldman Publishing Corporation.

Library of Congress Cataloging-in-Publication Data

Marko, Eve
  Clara Barton and the American Red Cross / by Eve Marko ; illustrations by Pablo Marcos.--Library ed.
      p. cm. -- (Heroes of America)
   Originally published: New York : Baronet Books, c1996.
   ISBN 1-59679-255-8
   1. Barton, Clara, 1821-1912. 2. American National Red Cross--Biography--Juvenile literature. 3. Nurses--United States--Biography--Juvenile literature. I. Marcos, Pablo. II. Title. III. Series.

HV569.B3M38 2005
361.7'634'092--dc22
[B]

                                                          2004063664

Table of Contents

Important Dates

1821   Clara Barton is born near North Oxford, Massachusetts.

1832   Clara nurses her injured brother, David.

1839   Clara starts 11 years of teaching school in Massachusetts.

1852   Clara establishes a free public school at Bordentown, New Jersey.

1854   Clara goes to Washington, D.C. and becomes a government clerk.

1861   Clara begins work as a nurse in the Civil War.

1865   Clara locates missing soldiers.

1869   Clara sails to Europe.

1870   Clara has her first meeting with leaders of the International Red Cross.

1873   Clara returns home to organize the American Red Cross.

1881   Clara leads Red Cross relief after fires, floods, hurricanes and earthquakes.

1884   Clara helps victims of the Ohio and Mississippi floods.

1912   Clara Barton dies in her home in Glen Echo, Maryland, on April 12.

Chapter 1

Learning from David

"Come on, Clara!" David Barton yelled over his shoulder at the young girl riding behind him. "Let's see if you can catch me!"

Clara Barton was only ten years old. Her brother David was twenty-three. But that wasn't going to stop her from riding as fast as or even faster than he could!

Holding the reins tight in her hand, she bent low till her head almost reached the horse's ears. "Come on, Blackie," she whispered. "Let's show

Racing Against the Wind

David how fast we can ride." Then she kicked the mare's haunches with her small feet.

But Blackie didn't need any help or reminder. She galloped fast, steam coming out of her nostrils as they rode across the cold, bare fields. It was winter in the year 1832 and the Massachusetts countryside was frozen and empty except for the two riders on their horses racing against the wind. In just a few minutes Clara came alongside her brother, and just a few minutes after that she passed him. Then she reined Blackie in and slowly stopped to let David catch up with her.

"I beat you!" she said, her dark eyes laughing.

"You beat me fair and square," David agreed. "But just remember one thing, Clara. If you ever have to ride fast, stretch forward as much as you can and keep your head low. If you sit up that will make you go slower."

Clara listened carefully. David was her riding

teacher. When she was five he'd taught her to ride bareback, with no saddle. Everything she knew about riding came from him.

David grinned. "Race you to French River," he said. And before Clara could say anything, he was off.

It didn't take Clara much time to catch up with him again. He was older and faster and he was riding his own horse, but Clara was small and light as a feather. She was practically one with the saddle and there was no stopping her now. It was late in December, a few days before Christmas, but so far the winter had been a mild one and there was little snow on the ground. Clara wished more snow would come soon, in time for Christmas.

Finally they got to French River, which ran down the hills and curved along the fields and meadows. David got off his horse. So did Clara.

"You beat me again," he told her. "But let's see

They Got to French River.

you do this."

David walked toward French River. Clara followed, curious and a little nervous. Her brother David loved to play games. Everything he did, he did well. He was the best horseback rider around. He was the best climber and ballplayer, too. He taught her how to do all these things. What was he going to show her now?

They came to the edge of French River. This was the narrowest point of the river. Somebody had put a long log across it so that the farmers who worked the fields could cross here. The log was hardly more than a foot wide.

"Follow me," David said. He put one foot on the log, then another, and then he started walking along the narrow log towards the other shore.

Clara didn't hesitate. She loved and trusted David more than anybody in the world. He was her best friend. She stepped on the log. The log began to sway back and forth. Suddenly, Clara felt afraid.

"Are you sure this is safe?" she asked.

David looked back over his shoulder. "Positive," he told her. "Just keep on walking and don't look down."

Clara did just what David said. She took one step, then another, then another. Ahead of her was David's big, broad back. Clara had three other brothers and sisters besides David. They were all much older than her and she loved them very much. But nobody was like David.

Clara took longer, bigger steps on the narrow log. David was way ahead of her and she wanted to catch up. It was too bad that the log was so narrow, she thought—otherwise she would have passed him here, too.

Just then David reached the edge of the log and stepped off. The log jerked violently up and down. Clara froze in her tracks. Suddenly she couldn't take

But Suddenly Clara Was Afraid.

another step.

"Come on, Clara!" David said. "Walk straight ahead. You won't fall!"

But suddenly Clara was afraid of falling. She looked down. The water was dark and deep.

"Don't look down!" David told her. "Look straight ahead and take one step after another. Don't look down and don't stop."

She raised her foot and took one step. The log under her feet shook and her foot trembled. But she took another step, and then another, and another. She kept her eyes straight ahead just like David had told her to. Beneath her feet the log was still shaking, but it didn't matter anymore. She had to keep on walking.

Clara's steps grew bigger and more confident. In no time at all she was on the other side. David caught her as she jumped off the log and then lifted her and swung her gently around.

"Hooray for Clara!" he shouted. "The bravest girl in the entire state of Massachusetts!"

Clara laughed. Her long, dark hair that had been tied with a ribbon fell loose all around her face. David put her down and she picked up the red ribbon from the ground. All her ribbons were red. Clara loved the color red.

"You learned an important lesson today, Clara," David said. "What did you learn?"

Clara thought hard. David always taught her to do things the proper way. He'd shown her the proper way to throw a ball and the proper way to catch it, the proper way to ride horses and the proper way to take care of them.

Clara smiled. "I learned to keep on walking, not look down— never give up!" she said.

David grinned. "Perfect," he said. "I couldn't have said it better."

Clara and David raced home, just as the sun

"What Did You Learn?"

was going down. "I wish the days were longer," Clara said happily as they came inside the house. "That way we could spend more time outdoors!"

"Right now I'm happy to see you *indoors*," Mrs. Barton said, coming out of the kitchen in her gingham apron and looking fondly at her youngest daughter. "I was waiting for you to help me bake a chocolate cake."

"Chocolate cake!" Clara exclaimed. Chocolate cake was her favorite dessert. But then her eyes fell. She didn't want to spend time in the kitchen when there were still so many games to play outdoors.

"I want you to help me bake the cake before your father comes home," Mrs. Barton said. "He went to the horse fair today and he'll be coming home tired and hungry. Besides, Clara, baking is very important. It's like cooking and darning socks and sewing. They may not seem as much fun as going riding or playing ball, but believe me, young lady, one day you'll find them very useful and you'll be glad you learned to do them. Anyway, don't you like licking the bowl after we've finished making the cake?"

Clara smiled. Suddenly she felt something by her leg. She looked down.

"Button!" It was her little white dog rubbing against her leg. When she looked down at him, he sat down and raised his front left paw. Immediately Clara noticed a red spot.

"Button, what happened?"

Clara sat down on the floor and held Button's paw, looking closely. Button trusted Clara; her hand was so gentle. "Oh, poor Button. He broke his toenail. He's bleeding." Clara looked up at her mother. "May I go upstairs to take care of Button? Then I'll come down and help you bake the cake."

"Of course you may," Mrs. Barton said, smiling. Everybody in the Barton family knew that Clara

Button Limped Up After Her.

loved to nurse little birds and animals back to health. She'd taken care of dogs, cats, birds— even raccoons.

"Come on, Button!" Clara started upstairs and Button limped up after her. She soaked his paw to clean off the blood and then put an ointment on it. When she finished, Clara went back downstairs, took out the big bags of flour and cocoa and started helping her mother with the baking.

Many years later Clara was to think back on how many things she'd done that winter day, just before Christmas: riding, nursing, and baking. One day in the future, those three things were going to mean the difference between life and death—not just for her, but for many, many people.

Chapter 2

Happy Birthday!

Clara and her mother were still in the kitchen an hour later, when suddenly Button barked and ran to the door. Clara looked out the window.

"Is that your father coming home?" Mrs. Barton asked.

"It's him!" Clara said excitedly. "And he's got a new horse with him!" She looked over her shoulder at her mother. "I know we haven't finished the cake yet, but can I go out now and finish it later?"

Her mother laughed. "Go right ahead. This is

"He's Got a New Horse!"

one chocolate cake I want to finish baking myself."

Clara put on her warm cloak and ran out the door. Her father had come out of the woods and was riding across the meadow toward the barn. His hair was already white but he still sat straight and tall in his saddle. The local farmers called him Captain Barton from the days when, as a young man, he'd fought in the Indian wars in Ohio and Michigan.

"How was the horse show?" she asked, looking up at him. "Were there many beautiful horses?"

"There sure were," her father said. He bent down and scooped her up onto his saddle.

"But you bought only one horse," Clara said, looking over his shoulder at the horse he was leading behind him.

"I bought the best horse in the fair," Captain Barton said. Together they rode into the barn where David was already waiting. He whistled appreciatively when he saw the new horse. "Well, what do you think?" David asked his sister with a big grin on his face. "Do you like him?"

"He's the most beautiful horse I've ever seen."

"I'm glad you think so," Captain Barton said with a smile, looking down at his daughter. "He's your birthday present, Clara. Two days from now, on Christmas Day, you're going to turn eleven years old. I think that's a good age to get your own horse."

"I'll take good care of him!" Clara replied with delight, putting her arms around the horse's neck. "I know he has to be brushed after I ride him. And I promise he'll get water and fresh hay every day."

"And if anything ever happens to one of his legs, that horse will have the best nurse in all of Massachusetts!" David added. "What are you going to call him, Clara?"

"Billy," Clara said right away, stroking Billy's silky mane.

"Billy's a good name," her father said. "And here

Father Took Down a Silver-Trimmed Saddle.

is another gift—from your mother. You'll need it if you're going to ride Billy." From a nail on the wall of the barn, Clara's father took down a silver-trimmed saddle.

"It's beautiful! A sidesaddle! The kind grown women use," Clara gasped.

"Your mother learned to ride on this saddle, and now she's giving it to you," her father said.

Clara ran to throw her arms around her mother, standing in the front doorway. "It's the most beautiful saddle I've ever seen!"

Her mother gave her a hug. "I came to get you all for dinner. You must be starved after the day you've all had. Stephen, Dorothy and Sally are home from work and dinner is on the table—so hurry up."

Clara led Billy into his stall. She brushed him, then gave him fresh hay and water. She even ran to the kitchen and brought back a few lumps of sugar for her new horse. What a wonderful day this was.

Riding with David, overcoming her fear of French River, and now Billy! Her very own horse!

Quickly she hurried back to the house. The whole family was sitting down to dinner. She gave a big hug to her brother and two sisters. But there were more surprises in store for Clara. At the end of dinner her mother brought out the chocolate cake she'd baked earlier that day. But it wasn't quite the usual cake. Her mother had put on the chocolate frosting and written "Happy Birthday, Clara" on it.

"I suggest we have dessert in front of the fire-place where we can all relax," Mrs. Barton said.

They did just that. The fire had already been lit to warm up the house. Outside they could hear the wind rattling the shutters. Snow was on the way.

"You're two days shy of eleven," Clara's sister Dorothy said. "Do you ever think of what you'd like to do when you grow up?"

"Oh, all the time," Clara said enthusiastically.

Dessert in Front of the Fireplace

Her dark eyes sparkled. "There's so much I want to do. I'd like to be a teacher, too, like you." Sally Stephen, and Dorothy had all become teachers.

"That's a good idea," Mrs. Barton said. "You three teach school, why not Clara, too?"

"I want to be a teacher," Clara said dreamily, gazing into the crackling logs in the fire, "but I want to be something else, too."

"What's that, Clara?" David asked her.

"I want to be a soldier."

"A *soldier*?" Captain Barton said, his eyebrows raised, smiling at his daughter. "Women aren't soldiers. Only men are soldiers."

"I want to be a soldier just like you," Clara said to her father. She got up and went to sit by him next to the fire. "I want to serve under famous generals and fight alongside the other soldiers, just like you did when you fought in the Indian wars."

"Is that why you ride so hard and try to do

everything the boys do, only better?" David asked. They all laughed at that. Outside the family Clara was shy, but at home she tried to do everything. She rode horses, she ice-skated, she'd even helped paint the house when she was only eight years old.

"I always loved hearing the stories you told me about the wars," Clara said to her father, leaning against his shoulder. "Remember the story of how you lay in the marshes in Michigan and all you had to drink was the muddy water from the marsh?"

"Clara knows all about generals, colonels, captains and sergeants," her father said. "I don't know another young girl who knows as much about soldiers and wars as she does."

"That's why I wish I could be a soldier, too," she said. "Just like you. Just like President Andrew Jackson. He was a great soldier before he became president."

"I'm afraid girls are never allowed on the bat-

"There's Always a First Time," She Said.

tlefield," her sister Dorothy told her. "Not even when they become grown-up women, Clara."

Clara looked dreamily into the fire again. "There's always a first time," she said, her voice trailing off.

Her brothers and sisters laughed, but not her father. He raised his hand, and the laughter quieted down.

"I wouldn't laugh so hard at what Clara said," he told them. "I think she means every word."

"I do!" Clara said eagerly.

"If that's the case," Captain Barton said, looking fondly at his daughter, "then you'll find the way. May God bless you and help you on your journey."

Chapter 3

David Gets Hurt

Christmas came and went. The winds died down, the snows melted, and one day Clara opened the shutters, looked out her window and saw a gray bird with an orange belly and a yellow bill, singing its song.

"A robin!" she exclaimed happily. "That means spring is here." She could hardly wait to be outdoors again.

But that year life held something very different in store for eleven-year-old Clara Barton—some-

"A Robin! Spring Is Here!"

thing that nobody expected.

Clara's father, Captain Barton, was building a new barn. It was a big job, so people's neighbors would all come to help. In those days, they called this a barn-raising. The men brought wood beams, ladders and axes while the women brought hampers full of good things to eat, along with apple cider and hot coffee. Raising a new barn was a hard day's work, but in the middle of the day people still made time for a big lunch with lots of talk and laughter.

Some people called out to Clara's brother. "Come on, David, get up to that ridgepole and get to work!"

Clara looked up to the ridgepole at the top of the new barn. Only the best athlete was asked to climb up to the ridgepole, the very top of the roof— the point—to fix the wooden rafters up that high. In North Oxford, where the Bartons lived, that meant only one person: David Barton.

CLARA BARTON

David started to climb up toward the ridgepole. "Be careful, David!" Clara cried out.

"Don't you worry, young lady," said a neighbor at her side. "Nobody knows how to climb the ridgepole like your brother."

David didn't seem concerned. Quickly he reached the high beam that connected the front and back walls of the barn. When he was at the very top he waved at Clara to show her he was all right. Then he walked across the narrow beam from one end to the other.

Suddenly there was a loud cr-r-r-ack! The high wooden beam broke apart in the middle. David fell from the top of the barn and with a sickening thud, he hit the ground.

"David!" Clara cried. She was the first to reach his side.

"David!" she whispered. She looked at his body, lying still on the ground. Was he terribly hurt? Was

Slowly He Sat Up.

he—dead?

But David opened his eyes. Slowly he sat up.

"Are you all right, David?" Clara asked, her heart in her mouth. Everybody else crowded around them, looking carefully at David.

"I'm all right," David said, rubbing his forehead with his hand. "Clara, don't look so worried. There's just a little pain behind my eyes—nothing serious. Now, Clara, don't tell me you're going to start crying!"

Clara shook her head. Crying wasn't going to help anyone. But she was worried about her big brother.

"Let's get back to work," David said, getting to his feet.

"What about that pain behind your eyes?" Mrs. Barton asked. She was worried, too.

"Probably just a small bruise. Nothing a grown man can't handle."

David got up and went back to work. But he didn't climb up to the ridgepole anymore that day.

A week later, David couldn't get out of bed.

"What's the matter, David?" Clara asked anxiously, standing by his bed, her eyes big with worry. Her older brother, David, the one she adored more than anybody else in the entire world, looked pale and tired.

"I feel so weak," David whispered. "I can't move. And it hurts so badly behind my eyes!"

Clara put her hands on her brother's forehead. It was hot and moist. "You have a fever," she told him. "I'm going to get some cold compresses." Quickly she got a basin of water and fresh linen towels.

Mrs. Barton hurried upstairs. One look at David's pale face and motionless body convinced his mother that this was serious. "We must get a doctor," she told him. "I'll take care of you in the mean-

"You Have a Fever."

time."

"Let me take care of David," Clara begged her mother. "I'll nurse him back to health."

"That could take a long time, Clara," her mother told her. "You have to go to school."

"I'm going to stay here as long as I need to," Clara said. She put the basin down by the bed and dipped the linens in the water, then gently laid the compresses across David's forehead. He groaned weakly, and whispered, "That feels good."

When Mrs. Barton saw this she didn't say another word. Instead, she hurried out to get the doctor.

Clara continued wetting David's hot forehead with the cold compresses. "You'll be fine," she told him.

"Just don't leave me," David whispered. "Your hands feel so good."

Once again, Clara almost felt like crying when

she saw how weak David was. But this was no time for tears. She was going to stay cheerful and hopeful for his sake.

The doctor came and brought with him ointments and medicine. He left specific instructions on how to administer the medicine, and how often. Clara wrote it all down very carefully. That evening she arranged a bed for herself right by David's.

"I'm not leaving you," she told him. "I'm going to be your nurse till you get well."

Night and day Clara stayed by David's side. Carefully she gave him the medicine the doctor left, making sure to follow the doctor's instructions.

The days turned warm and summer soon came. Sometimes Mrs. Barton came in and ordered Clara to go out for a breath of air, but Clara left unwillingly, returning as soon as she could.

Summer came and went. Soon it was fall again. Before long, Christmas was on its way and David

"I Can Cure Your Son."

was still bed-ridden.

"I'm never going to get well," her brother whispered sadly. "Even the doctors don't come back anymore. There are no more medicines. They say there's nothing more they can do."

"That isn't so," Clara said. She held his big hand tightly in her own tiny one. "I know you'll get healthy, and soon! One day you'll walk out of here and be your old self, and we'll race to French River just like we used to. I promise!"

David smiled when he heard this. Soon he turned his head and fell asleep. Clara straightened the bedcovers neatly around him and sat by his bed, never moving from his side.

Winter passed and spring came, and with the spring a new doctor arrived. He took one look at David and said to Captain Barton, "I can cure your son. But he must go to a sanitarium where he will get good treatment and lots of rest."

CLARA BARTON

"If David goes I must go with him," Clara protested.

The doctor smiled. "I know you haven't left your brother's side in more than a year. It's probably thanks to you that he's still alive. I wouldn't dream of separating you now."

So Clara went with David to the sanitarium, and after a month David was able to get out of bed. After another month he was walking, with Clara's help. All the doctors and nurses smiled to see the big man leaning on the small young girl as they walked down the grassy paths together.

One day Captain Barton and his wife came to fetch David and bring him home. He was on his feet, feeling fit and healthy, just as Clara had promised.

"Thank you so much, doctor," Mrs. Barton said. "You did miracles for our son."

"Don't thank me," the doctor said. "Thank Clara. She's the real miracle-worker. That girl is

"I Must Go With Him."

twelve years old, but I've never seen a more loyal, gentle, and dedicated nurse. It's thanks to Clara that David finally recovered."

David looked down at his little sister. She looked up at him. "I just knew you were going to make it," she whispered. "God wasn't going to take you away from me."

Chapter 4

School Teacher

After David recovered, Clara went back to school. When a few years had passed, she began to think again of teaching school herself.

"Sally, Dorothy and Stephen are schoolteachers," she said to David. "I think I'd like to teach school, too."

"Are you sure you're big enough?" he asked teasingly.

"I'm seventeen," she told him.

"I don't mean your age, Clara," he said, muss-

"I Have to Earn Their Respect."

ing up her hair. "I mean your size. Do you think those students are going to listen to you?" Clara was only five feet tall.

"They'll listen to me if they respect me," Clara told David. "I'll have to find a way to earn their respect."

Shortly after that she earned her first teaching certificate. One bright early morning in May, Clara Barton walked to the one-room schoolhouse near North Oxford. It was her first day as a teacher and she was nervous. She wore her new green dress with velvet trim. It reached all the way down to her shoes. Her thick, dark hair was parted in the middle with curls falling over her ears, which made her look like an adult. But did she feel like an adult? Could she act like an adult? She wasn't much older than many of her pupils, she knew. Some of them were going to be bigger than she was. Would they listen to her?

CLARA BARTON

Heart pounding with anticipation, Clara opened the door to the schoolhouse and entered. Forty heads turned around to look at her as she stood by the doorway. The children were already at their desks. Bright and rosy-cheeked, aged four to thirteen, they were all in one class and all pupils of Clara Barton.

"Good morning, boys and girls," Clara said as she made her way to the front of the room.

"Good morning, Miss Barton," they answered.

Her desk was on a raised platform in front of the class so that her students could see her. Clara Barton sat down and looked down at her pupils' faces.

"Do you each have a Bible?" she asked them.

Solemnly, they nodded.

"Please open to the book of Matthew, chapter five. We will study Jesus' Sermon on the Mount. Who would like to start reading? We'll take turns."

"Good Morning, Boys and Girls."

CLARA BARTON

One little girl raised her hand. "What's your name?" Clara asked, smiling.

"Emily," the little girl said.

"All right, Emily, you may begin."

Emily began reading earnestly, and the other pupils read silently along. Clara's sharp eyes soon noticed the pupil seated behind Emily. He was a big boy, bigger even than Clara, and though he pretended to read his Bible, he was actually laughing behind his hand and giving funny looks to three other boys who sat in the next row.

Clara knew this boy. His name was Pete Boyd. He and his three friends were the four biggest boys in the class. They were also bullies. She remembered they'd made a lot of trouble for the teacher last year. She would have to deal with them carefully but firmly.

During the break all the children went outside to play. Suddenly little Emily came running up to

Clara.

"Pete's hurt, Miss Barton," she cried. "Please come right away!"

Clara hurried over to the schoolyard behind the schoolhouse. In the yard lay Pete Boyd with a big scratch on his cheek. Next to him stood his three friends.

"What happened?" Clara demanded.

One of the other big boys mumbled, then laughed. But when Clara raised herself to her full height, eyes blazing, and demanded again to know what happened, he turned red and said, "We were pitching horseshoes, Miss Barton. I pitched one and hit Pete in the face."

Quickly Clara bent over Pete Boyd. Her two year's experience nursing David was already to her advantage. She looked knowledgeably at the scratch and said, "You're lucky, Pete. There is a little blood, but it's dried already. It's nothing that a clean hand-

"*You*, Miss Barton, to Pitch Horseshoes?"

kerchief and a little water can't fix." Clara gave him her own handkerchief and told him to wash his face and come back. The big boy looked at the young teacher with curiosity, but then did as he was told.

When he came back Clara said to the four boys, "From now on, whenever you pitch horseshoes you must make sure everybody stands far away from the peg. That way no one will get hurt. Your concentration will be better and your scores will be higher. Here—give me the horseshoes and I'll show you."

Pete Boyd looked at Clara, his mouth wide open. "*You*, Miss Barton? You want to pitch horseshoes?"

"I'm not only going to pitch horseshoes, Pete," Clara said with a smile, "I'm going to show you how to do it right."

Still astonished, the big boy gave her the horseshoes. But that was nothing, compared to his surprise when Clara pitched them. Pete bent over to examine the horseshoes as they lay neatly around the peg, then looked up, flabbergasted. "You didn't miss *one*, Miss Barton!" he exclaimed. "You have a perfect score!" He'd never met a teacher like this in his entire life.

But that was only the beginning. The next day during recess Clara Barton played ball with the big boys, and very quickly they discovered that she could throw and catch better than any of them. Soon she was not only teaching them how to spell and how to do arithmetic, but also how to jump to catch a ball thrown high or wide, and how to throw straight. Even in her long dresses and wide skirts, Clara could run and jump better than any of them.

Those boys never made trouble for Clara again. They became her best pupils. They learned to read and write. They also learned history and geography. And Clara had earned their respect—just as she'd promised David she would do.

"You Didn't Miss One!"

Chapter 5

Bordentown

Clara Barton taught school in Massachusetts for thirteen years. Some of her pupils grew up, got married and had children, and then Clara even taught those children, too. Whenever they returned to visit her, no matter how big and grown-up they'd become, Clara Barton always called them "my children." She thought of all her pupils as her own children—every single one.

In 1850 Clara decided it was time for her to be a student again, not just a teacher, so she went to study further at a teachers' institute in Clinton, New York.

Two years later she decided it was time for a short vacation. So one beautiful day in late spring, Clara traveled to the town of Bordentown, New Jersey, to see her friend Mary Norton. The two young women planned to spend three weeks together, talking, walking, picnicking and just having fun. But one day as they walked in the streets of Bordentown, Clara stopped in her tracks.

"That's funny," she said. "Look, Mary."

Mary looked, then turned to her friend. "I don't see anything."

"Yes, you do," Clara replied. "Look again."

Mary looked across the street and said, "I just see three boys on the other side of the street, Clara."

"That's just it, Mary. What are these young boys doing on the street on a weekday? They're supposed to be in school!"

"There Is No School for Me."

CLARA BARTON

Without waiting for an answer, Clara walked over to one of the boys who was standing on the corner with his friends. "Young man," she said, "aren't you supposed to be in school right now?"

The boy looked at the pretty woman standing in front of him. "Maybe I'm supposed to be, miss," he said, "but there is no school for me."

"No school for you!" Clara exclaimed. "I've never heard of such a thing. In this country there are supposed to be schools for all boys and girls. That's the law. What's your name?"

"My name's Jeremy Hart. And there are no schools for me and my friends in Bordentown," the boy told her. "We're too poor. They think we would only cause trouble if we went to school."

From the corner of her eye Clara noticed Jeremy's clothes. They were old and worn. The pants were scruffy, the shirtsleeves torn beneath the elbows.

Her face softened. She held out her hand and touched his arm. "Jeremy, if there were a school for you and your friends, would you go?"

Jeremy's face lit up immediately. "Oh, yes! I want to learn how to read and write. I want to learn how to do sums. Otherwise I'll end up poor, just like my father."

"I'll open up a school for you," Clara said. "And I'll teach you reading and writing and arithmetic myself. That's a promise."

The boys whooped and hollered with excitement when they heard this.

"Mary, I want you to introduce me to the school committee of Bordentown," Clara told her friend. "I want to talk to them about opening a school for these children. School can't be just for children from rich families. School is for every child, rich or poor."

"But, Clara," Mary said, "you're here to have a vacation, not start a new school!"

"I'll Open a School for You."

"Mary, I can't have a vacation while these children are out on the street," Clara said, looking very determined. "It makes my blood boil!"

That very afternoon Clara met with the small group of gentlemen who ran the schools in Bordentown.

"Young boys like Jeremy Hart shouldn't be out on the street," Clara told them. "They should be going to school like all other American children."

"Jeremy Hart and his friends are no good," one man from the committee told her. "Their parents are poor and the boys are troublemakers."

"All children should have a chance to learn no matter how much money their parents have," Clara replied. "I've talked with these boys and I don't think they're troublemakers.

"And just to prove it," Clara added, "I'm prepared to open that school and teach it myself."

The committee members looked at her in astonishment. "If you give me a schoolhouse where I can hold classes, I will teach those children free of charge for the entire year," Clara said.

"But you're a young woman!" another committee member said. "And you're a stranger in Bordentown. Those boys will never listen to you. I tell you—they're troublemakers."

"I've been teaching in Massachusetts for thirteen years," Clara said spiritedly, "and in those thirteen years my pupils have taught me as much as I've taught them. One of the things they've taught me is that children are the same everywhere, and they all want to learn. If I can teach in Massachusetts, I can teach in Bordentown. If you give me the schoolhouse I *will* teach these children. You'll see!"

The committee members looked at each other. They'd never met a teacher like this before.

They talked it over and finally told Clara, "Miss Barton, you have a deal. We will give you a school-

Only Six Boys Came That First Day.

house provided you teach the classes. But we warn you—you're asking for a lot of trouble. These children won't learn. In fact, we don't even think they'll come to class. But if you're ready to try, we'll help you."

On the first day of school, Clara opened the schoolhouse and waited, full of excitement and anticipation. To her disappointment, only six boys came that first day. One of them was Jeremy Hart.

"How do you like your new school, Jeremy?" she asked him.

"I like it fine, Miss Barton," he answered with a grin.

"Then tell your friends, Jeremy. Tell them that if they want to learn and get ahead, they have to come to school."

"I'll tell them," Jeremy promised. "You kept your promise, Miss Barton. You opened a school for us. They'll come, Miss Barton. They want to learn, same as I do."

Jeremy was right. The word soon spread that there was a school open for all the poor children. More and more young boys and girls came to school every day.

Clara taught in Bordentown just as she had taught in Massachusetts. She taught her children not only reading and writing, not only arithmetic and geography—she also played games with them, helped them with their homework and visited their families. By the end of the year six hundred children were coming to school. The old schoolhouse was no longer big enough for all of them. Clara Barton had so much work on her hands that she had to persuade more teachers to help her.

"You've done the best job any teacher has ever done in the city of Bordentown, Miss Barton," the school committee told her. "Nobody ever managed to teach these children anything before, yet you came

She Visited Their Families.

in and did it all by yourself."

The school committee decided to open a new and bigger school. But Clara was exhausted. One day she came to the schoolhouse, faced the children and opened her mouth to start teaching—but nothing came out.

"You're completely worn out," the doctor told her that evening after examining her. "You've lost your voice because you need a rest. A nice long one, too. Go someplace new—someplace you've never been before."

Clara Barton thought it over. "I've always wanted to go to Washington, D.C.," she told her friend Mary Norton. "Maybe I could get a job there."

"But that's so far from here, Clara!"

"My sister Sally is now living in Washington. I can rest at her house for a while before I find new work."

"New work?" Mary said. "Don't you want to go

on teaching? You're the best teacher we ever had in Bordentown."

"I've been a schoolteacher for over fifteen years," Clara said thoughtfully. "Maybe it's time to do something new. And if I'm going to do something new with my life, something I've never done before, what better place to do it than in our nation's capital?"

So Clara went to Washington, D.C. She was right. A new life was waiting for her, something she'd never done before; something no woman in America had ever done before.

It took six more years for that to happen—six years, to the beginning of the American Civil War.

To See the New President

Chapter 6

Civil War

"Are we there yet, Aunt Clara?" Stephen Barton asked excitedly.

Stephen was tall for fourteen, and he walked fast, but he practically had to run to keep up with his aunt.

"We're almost there, Stephen," Clara said, slowing down a little. The streets in Washington, D.C. were still unpaved and it was easy to slip and fall, particularly on a day like today when so many people had come out to see the new president.

CLARA BARTON

It was March 4, 1860. Inauguration Day. The day was cold but clear, with bright sunlight. People hurried alongside them.

After six years of living in Washington, Clara really loved the city. It was still not finished. Most of the government buildings had not yet been constructed, and the streets were often muddy. Clara loved nothing more than to go down to the Capitol building after she finished work and listen to the arguments of senators and representatives from all over the country as they debated the future of the United States.

She loved copying secret papers in the U.S. Patent Office where she now worked as a copy clerk. It was different from teaching, and Clara Barton was happy.

But today promised to be the most exciting day of all. A new president was going to be sworn in on the steps of the Capitol. His name was Abraham

Clara Really Loved the City.

Lincoln.

"There's the Capitol," Clara said to her nephew, pointing to a building with two wings that still had no roofs. "Once it's finished, the House of Representatives will meet there." She pointed. "And the Senate will meet there. It doesn't look like much now," she said with a smile, "but you wait till it's finished. It'll be the most beautiful building in the country."

"Look at how many people are standing below the steps!" Stephen exclaimed.

"They've come just like us to watch Mr. Lincoln be sworn in."

A large black carriage rolled slowly down Pennsylvania Avenue and made its way towards the Capitol. In it sat Abraham Lincoln and his wife, Mary Todd Lincoln.

"He's so tall, Aunt Clara!" Stephen exclaimed.

That's true, Clara thought when she saw Abraham Lincoln for the first time. *He's tall and thin.*

CLARA BARTON

But he looks so sad.

As the carriage passed on its way to the Capitol the crowds cheered and waved to the new President. But he didn't wave back.

"He looks like he has something on his mind, Aunt Clara," Stephen said.

"I'm afraid he does," Clara said thoughtfully.

Even as she said this, she heard the shout of a newspaper boy as he hawked the newspapers in his hand. "Lincoln inaugurated today! Southern troops surround Fort Sumter! Read all about it!"

"Is anything the matter, Aunt Clara?" Stephen asked.

"Something is very much the matter," Clara said, biting her lip. Her big black eyes, usually full of fun and laughter, were now serious—even sad. "These are very difficult times for our country."

"Is there going to be a war, Aunt Clara?"

"I don't know, Stephen. When Abraham Lincoln

"Lincoln Disapproves of Slavery."

won the election last fall, seven Southern states withdrew from the United States—seceded, and proclaimed their independence. They call themselves the Confederate States of America."

"Why, Aunt Clara?"

"Because the people in those seven states own slaves," Clara explained. "Abraham Lincoln disapproves of slavery, as do many other Americans in the Northern states. Lincoln wants the country to do away with—abolish—slavery. But slaveowners in the Southern states refuse. It's against our constitution to secede, but those states have left the Union."

Clara looked at Stephen. He was only 14, still too young to understand how terrible a war could be. Suddenly tears came to her eyes. In several years Stephen would be old enough to serve in the army like so many other young men. He might get hurt. He might even die.

"I still hope there won't be war, Stephen," she said. "I'm sure that's what Mr. Lincoln hopes, too."

Suddenly they heard great cheering and applause. They looked up. Abraham Lincoln was walking up the steps of the Capitol toward a man wearing a black robe.

"What are they doing now, Aunt Clara?" Stephen asked, very excited.

"The man in the black robe is Roger Taney," Clara explained. "He's the Chief Justice of the United States Supreme Court, and he will administer the Oath of Office to the new president."

The two watched as Abraham Lincoln put one hand on a Bible and raised the other hand. They couldn't hear the words because the people were applauding and cheering, but Clara knew that when Abraham Lincoln lowered his hand, put the Bible down, and shook hands with Chief Justice Roger Taney, he had just become the sixteenth President

Lincoln Was Walking Up the Steps.

of the United States.

Then Abraham Lincoln stepped forward. He talked to the crowd standing below him. He talked about the importance of keeping the United States one country, one Union. He also called for peace, not war. That day Lincoln said, "We are not enemies, but friends. We must not be enemies. Though passion may have strained, it must not break our bonds of affection."

Clara again had tears in her eyes. Abraham Lincoln had spoken aloud the thoughts she had had for many months. She looked at the new president as he stood atop the steps of the Capitol, accepting the applause of the crowd around him. But his face was still solemn. *Such heavy responsibilities are on his shoulders,* Clara thought. How she wished she could help him! How she wished she could help keep the country out of war.

But there was little Clara Barton—or anybody,

for that matter—could do. Right after the inauguration of President Abraham Lincoln, South Carolina sent soldiers to attack Fort Sumter. The few U.S. soldiers in the fort held out as long as they could, but finally they had to surrender. The Southern army had many more soldiers and many more weapons.

On April 14, 1861, Fort Sumter was taken over by South Carolina. The next day President Lincoln issued a call throughout the North for 75,000 soldiers to halt the rebellion in the South.

The Civil War had begun.

"I'll Help Soldiers."

Chapter 7

She's on Her Way

"I'm well and strong and young," Clara Barton wrote in her diary when the Civil War began. "If I can't be a soldier, I'll help soldiers."

But not everybody felt the same way. Washington, D.C. was part of the South, just across the Potomac River from Virginia, which had also seceded from the Union and joined the Confederacy. That meant that Confederate soldiers were just across the river from the capital of the United States. They could attack at any moment.

CLARA BARTON

Many people left Washington. But President Lincoln didn't leave. Instead he immediately asked for soldiers from the Northern states to come down to defend Washington. The 6th Massachusetts Regiment arrived by train. And when it did, Clara Barton was at the station to meet them.

As the soldiers stepped off the train, Clara saw a face that was familiar to her from long ago.

"Pete Boyd!" she exclaimed. "Do you remember me?"

The man looked at her closely. He was many years older than the boy Clara had taught years earlier, but Clara never forgot the faces of her students. A big smile appeared on his face. "Sure I remember you! You're Miss Barton! You taught us how to pitch horseshoes at the North Oxford schoolhouse!"

Clara laughed. "I hope that wasn't the only thing you learned from me, Pete," she said, giving him a big hug.

"Pete Boyd! Do You Remember Me?"

"There are some others here you'll remember," he told her eagerly. "Hey, men!" he shouted. "Look who's here. It's Miss Barton!"

The other men crowded around them and Clara recognized many of them. They'd been her pupils in Massachusetts, young boys she had taught how to read and write, now all grown up and ready to fight—maybe even die—for their country. Clara felt tears come to her eyes.

"All of you are a lot bigger than I remember," Clara said, "but you're still my boys and I'm still going to take care of you. Is there anything you need?"

"When we stopped in the Baltimore train station we were attacked by a mob," another soldier told her. "They killed a couple of our men—and wounded many others."

"You might say we're the lucky ones," Pete Boyd said. "We made it, all right, but we have nothing. We lost our clothes, our baggage, everything."

"We haven't had anything to eat, either," somebody else told her.

"I'll take care of that," Clara Barton promised them immediately. "I took care of you in school, and now that you've come down to Washington to defend this city, I'll take care of you again. Where are you boys staying?"

"They're putting us in the Capitol for now, before they send us to the front lines."

Clara Barton swung into action. She went back home and took out all the extra linens she had. She even tore up sheets to make handkerchiefs. She asked her neighbors for their extra linens, clothes and food, and packed everything in large baskets. The next day she came into the Senate Chamber of the Capitol where her soldiers were staying, followed by five porters carrying the enormous baskets of food and other supplies.

The Vice President's Chair

CLARA BARTON

Her boys whooped and hollered when they saw her. The soldiers of the regiment helped themselves to everything Clara had brought, joking and teasing with her, and she laughed right back. *This feels just like the old days,* Clara thought.

"I brought one more thing," she told them, her eyes twinkling as they ate hungrily.

"I got one copy of our newspaper from our old town, the *Worcester Spy!* I thought you might want to know what's happening back home."

The soldiers gave Clara Barton a cheer. They carried her toward the front of the Senate Chamber and placed her in the big chair reserved for the Vice President of the United States. Clara laughed, but she sat down. Then, in a loud, slow voice, she read the newspaper articles out loud to all the soldiers. They sat there and listened quietly as she read about events back home, picnics and barbecues, weddings and babies.

They thought of the girlfriends and wives they'd left behind, their children and their parents. And when Clara finished they gave her a standing ovation, whooping and carrying on as never before.

But Clara wasn't finished. She realized now how many things soldiers needed: towels, soap, needles, thread, linens, books! Not just her soldiers from Massachusetts, but all the Union soldiers from all over the North would need help. That very day she sat down and wrote letters to newspapers around the country, asking all the readers to send these supplies to her. She would then see to it that they were distributed fairly and evenly.

Soon Clara's home was filled with clothing, and cans of food, blankets and pillows, everything a soldier needed. She gave these to the soldiers as soon as she got them.

But soon something else bothered Clara. The North and the South had fought the battle of Bull

Soon Clara's Home Was Filled.

Run, and the North had lost. Clara and her sister Sally stood on the banks of the Potomac River as the wounded soldiers were brought back to Washington, where the nearest hospitals were. She watched as the soldiers lay in the sun or the rain, sometimes for hours, sometimes for days, waiting till they could be taken to the hospital. Clara did whatever she could—bandaging their wounds, feeding them—but often the soldiers died before her eyes.

"If there had been a nurse at the battlefield she could have taken care of the wounded soldiers right away. I bet most of these soldiers would still be alive today if someone had been there to bandage their wounds and feed them and keep them warm when they got hurt!" Clara told her sister.

"But nurses are women," Sally reminded her. "And women are never allowed near the battlefield."

"It's time they were," Clara said, looking at the wounded soldiers all around them. Many of them, she knew, were not going to make it to the end of the day. If only they had received treatment earlier!

"But where are you going to find nurses ready to risk their lives at the front lines?" Sally asked.

"There's one right here," Clara told her. "I want to go to the front lines to take care of our soldiers."

As soon as she got home, Clara wrote letters to the Union army asking permission to go to the front lines to nurse wounded soldiers. Finally she was given an appointment with a Union general.

"I would like to serve as a nurse at the battle-front," Clara told him.

"You?" the general said. "A woman?"

"Why not?" Clara said. "Those boys are fighting and getting hurt day after day. If they had somebody nursing them right away, instead of having to wait for days till they're brought back to a hospital in Washington, many of them would live."

"There is something in what you say," the gen-

"I Can't Send a Woman to the Battlefield."

eral said. "But I can't send a woman out to the battlefield. A woman's place is in the home."

But Clara wouldn't give up. She knocked on more doors, she talked to everybody she met. She believed she could go to the front to nurse wounded soldiers.

And then, in the middle of her efforts, she received bad news. Her father was ill back home.

Quickly, Clara went home to Massachusetts. Her father was 88 years old and Clara knew that he would soon die. She stayed to nurse him for several months, and during that time she told him what she wished to do.

Lying in his bed, Captain Barton held his daughter's hand and told her, "Go, if you belive it is your duty to go. I know soldiers, and they will respect you and your mission."

That gave Clara renewed strength and hope. When she returned to Washington she met Major

Rucker, who was in charge of making sure that the Union army had all the food and medical supplies it needed.

"I know I'm a woman," she told him, "but I'm strong and I'm not afraid. Soldiers are dying every day—soldiers who would still be alive if I were at their side. How many soldiers have to die before I will be permitted to serve my country in the best way I can?"

"Not many more," Major Rucker told her. "You're a brave woman, Miss Barton. If you're prepared to go to the front lines and face enemy fire and hardship, then that's what you should do."

Clara returned home, overjoyed. That evening when she visited her sister, she said, "Sally, I have the feeling that in just a short while I will finally be doing what I was destined to do. Do you remember that evening just before my birthday, the time you asked me what I was going to do when I grew up?"

"I'm Strong and I'm Not Afraid."

"You said you wanted to be a soldier and we all laughed," Sally said, smiling at that memory. "We didn't know how determined you could be. But don't forget, Clara, you were also a schoolteacher for many years, and a very good one."

"I was," Clara agreed. "But I think that I will be an even better nurse."

"Aren't you afraid?" Sally asked her then. "Aren't you afraid to be so close to the enemy, near big cannons and gunfire? No other American woman has ever gone so close to the battle lines."

Clara turned serious. "I'll probably be afraid when I get there, Sally. I'm sure the soldiers are afraid, too, but that doesn't prevent them from doing their best. And fear won't prevent me, either. I'll be the best nurse they ever had," she said, looking more determined than ever. "I want to save lives."

That summer Clara finally got a letter from the Surgeon General of the Union army, authorizing her

CLARA BARTON

to go to the front lines to nurse the Union soldiers.

Clara Barton was on her way. Of all the important steps she had taken already, of all the things she had done in her life so far, she was about to embark on the most significant undertaking of her life, for herself and for the world.

Wounded Soldiers Lay Everywhere.

Chapter 8

A Place Called Chantilly

Two months passed—the longest two months in Clara Barton's life.

Clara stood on a hilltop. It was nighttime; she'd lost track of the hour. In the surrounding darkness she could see nothing, but she could hear well enough. What she heard were the sickening moans and cries of the wounded.

Wounded soldiers lay everywhere, on slopes and in gullies, beneath the trees, and on the grass. The entire hillside was covered with them.

"I knew our brave soldiers needed me here," Clara said softly to herself, "but I never knew it would be like this!"

She was so tired she could hardly remember where she was. All she knew was that it was a place called Chantilly, somewhere in the state of Virginia.

She heard a moan nearby. "Miss Barton!"

Quickly she went back to work. She had bread in one bag slung over her shoulder, and held a big bucket of soup in her other hand. She also held a candle to light her way. She bent down and gently lifted up the wounded soldier's head, dipping a slice of bread in the soup and putting it in his mouth.

"God bless you," he said to her, looking up at the beautiful face of the woman bending over him.

"You'll be fine," Clara told him. "Soon the train will come to take you to the hospital in Washington. Have courage!"

"Thank you, Miss Barton," the soldier whis-

"God Bless You," He Said.

pered back to her. Clara looked like an angel of God to him, with the gentle smile that never left her face and the strong, busy hands that could support the shoulders of even the biggest and strongest soldier in the army.

Clara went further down the hill, stopping for each soldier. Down in the valley she could see her helpers making more soup in big pots over an open fire. But the winds were so bad, the smoke blew into their faces. They could hardly see.

There's a storm coming, Clara thought, worried. It was the last thing they needed right now.

She bent over a young boy, his shirt ripped into shreds over his chest. Suddenly, to her amazement, he wrapped an arm around her neck. "Don't you know me?" he whispered to her.

Clara looked at him in the faint light of the candle. There wasn't enough light to see.

"I'm Charlie Hamilton," he said to her. "You

were my teacher and I used to carry your bag home from school."

"Charlie Hamilton!" Clara exclaimed. "Of course I remember you."

Quickly she opened the bandage over Charlie's right shoulder. She could see that it needed to be replaced soon, otherwise the wound would get infected. She put down her soup and bread, took bandages out of her ample pockets and began to wrap up the wound.

"Tell me the truth, Miss Barton," Charlie said to her when she finished. Clara bent low over him. "Am I going to make it, Miss Barton? Please tell me the truth."

Clara felt tears coming to her eyes. She took a deep breath and made a big effort, and the tears didn't come. "Yes, Charlie," she said in a tender voice, "I believe you *will* make it. You will live. But if you want the full truth, I'm afraid you won't be

"I'll Carry It with My Left Arm."

able to carry my bag again with your right arm. You might not be able to carry anything with that arm any more. I'm very, very sorry—my dear Charlie."

A smile came over Charlie's face. "Then I'll carry it with my left arm, Miss Barton," he said.

Clara laughed with him and kissed him on the cheek before laying his head gently down on the ground again. How courageous he was, how gallant and strong and patient! He was one of "her children," the young pupils she had taught years ago in Massachusetts. Who would have thought she would meet those same children, now grown up, here on the fields of battle?

She continued on her way, bending over wounded soldiers, dipping bread into the soup and putting it into their mouths. She put socks and slippers on their cold, wet feet and wrapped them in blankets to keep them warm in the cold night air. How grateful they were for every little thing! Time and again they looked into her eyes and said, "God bless you, Miss Barton!"

In the morning the wounded would be put on a train to be taken to a hospital in Washington. It would be at least 24 hours before they were treated. If not for the nursing they received from Clara Barton, most of these soldiers wouldn't have been alive by the time the trains reached Washington.

"Miss Barton!"

She looked up and saw a doctor coming up the hill with a candle, looking for her.

She hurried toward him. "What is it, doctor?"

"Come quickly, Miss Barton," the doctor said. "There's a young boy lying on the other side of the hill. He's badly hurt."

"What's happened to him?" Clara asked, hurrying along.

"He keeps crying for his sister," the doctor told her. "He's badly wounded in the stomach, Miss Bar-

A Doctor Coming Up the Hill

ton. I don't think he'll live long. But his cries for his sister just break my heart!"

As soon as she approached the boy, Clara could hear the cries: "Mary, Mary—come! I'm wounded, Mary! Oh, Mary—please come!"

The doctor was right. The cries were so heartrending that Clara stopped in her tracks, tempted to turn around and run back. This was the second battle in which she was nursing the sick. In her worst dreams, Clara never imagined it would be like this. So many wounded, so many hurt and dying!

He's so young, Clara thought when she saw him. *He's hardly old enough to be a soldier.*

"Mary!" he cried. "Mary! Please come!"

Clara knelt by him in the darkness. She said nothing. Instead, she put her arms around his neck, kissed his cold forehead and laid her cheek against his.

CLARA BARTON

Suddenly a smile appeared on the boy's face. "Oh, Mary!" he exclaimed with joy. "I knew you would come if I called you!"

Clara wrapped his feet closely in blankets to keep him warm. Then she lifted his face onto her lap, gave him some hot soup and gently told him to rest.

"Bless you, bless you, Mary!" the boy said, still thinking that Clara was his sister.

Clara held him still. One hour passed, then another. Clara knew there were many other soldiers waiting for her, needing her services. But this boy kept on calling her Mary. The thought that his sister was holding him in her lap made him so happy that Clara couldn't bear to leave. She continued to sit there, holding his head gently.

Finally, after three hours had passed, the boy fell asleep. When Clara put his head carefully down on the ground, a smile was on his lips.

"I Can't Save That Boy's Life."

CLARA BARTON

"I don't believe he will ever wake up," the doctor whispered to Clara.

"At least he fell asleep thinking his sister had come to him," Clara said. "See how happily and sweetly he sleeps now!"

"You're a miracle-worker, Miss Barton," the doctor said.

"Not a miracle-worker, doctor," Clara answered. "I can't save that boy's life. But at least I can help him die with less pain and with more peace."

The doctor left and Clara looked at the hills in the distance. It was already getting light. She hadn't slept a wink that past night, nor would she be able to sleep today, for today there was going to be a big battle. That meant that by the afternoon more wounded would be brought to her, more soldiers needing her help.

Who will win this battle? she wondered. *The North? The South?* She wished the North would win so the war would end. No more bloodshed, no more death, no more wounded soldiers crying out, needing her help.

But the war wasn't going to end yet, and that meant she had a job to do. She had to be right here, ready with bandages, food, drink and encouragement, whenever they needed her.

She Had a Job to Do.

Chapter 9

Angel of the Battlefield

Clara's intuition was right. It *was* a bad day. Wounded soldiers started arriving by late morning. She was so busy taking care of them, she had no time to ask anybody what was happening at the front. But the sight of so many wounded soldiers told her the news wasn't good.

At three o'clock in the afternoon the last train carrying wounded soldiers to Washington was about to leave.

"Miss Barton," the doctor told her, "I think it

would be good for you to go on this train, too."

"I hear there'll be another battle this evening," Clara told him. "That means there will be more wounded soldiers who'll need my help."

"I'm afraid that's true," the doctor said, "but this time it can be very dangerous for you as well. The truth is, Miss Barton, we had a bad day today. It looks as if tonight the Confederate soldiers will break through the front lines and overrun us. That'll put all of us in danger, including you. Our soldiers will have to retreat. It's best if you go on the train back to Washington right now."

"I'm not leaving, doctor," Clara told him with quiet determination.

The doctor smiled tiredly at Clara, shaking his head with admiration. "I understand why our soldiers call you 'Angel of the Battlefield,' Miss Barton. You're the best nurse I've ever known. No wonder they love you as much as they do!"

Cannon and Artillery Fire

Quickly Clara went to the big pots she'd prepared with soup and stew. She hadn't eaten or rested in two days and she knew she would need all her strength for what was coming. But just as she dipped her bowl into the soup, a tremendous flash of lightning and a loud thunderbolt crashed across the skies. At that same moment there was the sound of an explosion from far away, then another, and another. The battle had begun.

The storm made the sky so black, Clara could see the flashing of cannon and artillery fire even though it was far away. The rain came pouring down.

"We have no more food for the soldiers," one of Clara's helpers told her.

"Do we have any food left at all?" Clara asked.

"Just army crackers," she was told.

"We'll put the crackers into knapsacks and beat them into crumbs, then add some wine and water and sweeten the crumbs with brown sugar," Clara said immediately.

The wounded soldiers who lay in the cold rain under wet blankets were grateful to receive this sweet mouthful from Clara as she made her way among them, never resting once. But the ground had turned into terrible mud. Clara slipped and fell countless times as she walked up and down the slopes among the wounded men.

In the morning Clara looked up and saw her soldiers, her beloved soldiers walking toward her, looking at the ground.

"We're retreating," one soldier told her gloomily. "We can't hold the lines. The Confederate soldiers will be here soon. You better come with us."

"I'm not leaving until all the wounded are taken care of," Clara said.

In her heart she was sick with sadness and disappointment. They had lost this battle. Everyone

Looking at the Ground

was tired and many were hurt. Was this war ever going to end?

At three o'clock in the afternoon an officer came galloping down on his horse toward her, bringing another horse with him. "Miss Barton, can you ride?" he asked quickly.

"I can ride as well as I can walk," Clara told him.

"In that case take this horse," he said, pointing to the horse he'd brought with him. "The last train is leaving the station immediately. Enemy soldiers have broken over the hills and are coming this way. Take this horse and ride towards the station as fast as you can."

Without waiting another minute, he offered his arm to Clara. Clara took one last look around. The wounded soldiers had all been taken to the station and put on the train to Washington. Now she could finally leave.

CLARA BARTON

"Now ride, Miss Barton! Ride as fast as you can!" he shouted, leading the way.

Clara galloped after him. The mud on the ground made it hard for the horse to go fast. Clara could feel herself sliding, even half falling off his back. But she kept her balance on the horse even without a saddle, and inside she blessed her brother David for teaching her to ride bareback on a horse so long ago.

Clara rode hard after the officer, and behind her she could hear the Confederacy's artillery, now louder than ever as they came down the hills. They rounded the bend and saw the train station. It was in flames. And there was the last train to Washington, already on its way.

"Ride, Miss Barton!" the officer shouted over his shoulder. "If we ride hard we'll overtake the train!"

Clara dug her heels into the horse's flanks and rode as hard as she could. The ground was treach-

They Overtook the Train.

erous and muddy, but the horse kept its balance. Before long they overtook the last car of the train. A conductor looked out of the window. When he recognized Clara Barton he slowed down the train. But he couldn't stop completely. That was too dangerous.

Clara and the officer rode alongside the moving train. Immediately dozens of arms came out to grab her. Clara rode alongside the door to one of the cars and held out her arm. Someone grabbed it and held hard. Without hesitating she swung over the horse toward the train. More arms came out, grabbed her and lifted her aboard.

The officer continued riding.

"Aren't you coming with us?" Clara shouted after him.

"I go with the army," the officer yelled. "Good luck, Miss Barton!" And he turned around and rode in the direction of the retreating Northern army. She wondered if she would ever see him again to thank him for saving her life.

Clara leaned against the window as the train picked up speed. Sometime tomorrow they would arrive in Washington and she would hurry home where she could finally wash, eat something and rest.

One day, she thought to herself, looking at the hills speeding by, *the fighting will stop, and then I will rest for a long time. But until that day I must work on and on. I must save the lives of our soldiers. I can't stop until they do.*

One Day the Fighting Will Stop.

Chapter 10

Fredericksburg

It was December. Soon it was going to be Christmas. Clara Barton stood on the second floor of an old colonial mansion in Falmouth, Virginia, and looked out the window.

"I've never seen so much snow in all my life," George told her. George was Clara's driver and helper. He drove Clara with all the supplies she needed from one battlefield to another.

"In Massachusetts, where I come from, we have even much more snow than here," Clara said with a smile. "Decembers are really cold up there."

But Decembers in Massachusetts also had Christmas and family and presents, Clara thought a little sadly. Christmas was also her birthday. She'd hoped to be in Washington for Christmas and her birthday, but now she wasn't sure that would happen. There was going to be a battle here soon and she would be needed.

She looked around her. "Do you think this place is big enough for all the wounded soldiers?" she asked George.

"This place? This is a mansion! There are twelve big rooms here. Plenty of space."

But Clara wasn't sure. She had the feeling that this was going to be a hard battle. That's why she'd brought along six army wagons filled with bandages, blankets, and food, not to mention plenty of assistants to help her. She looked around her at the old mansion called the Lacy House. For two days

Union Soldiers Running to the River

she had worked night and day to make a hospital out of it, and now she was ready. She looked out the window at the Rappahannock River, just outside the mansion.

"Are you looking at the Confederate soldiers on the other side of the river?" George said to her. "Don't look too closely or they might shoot."

Clara laughed. "They're a little too far away for that," she said. But her eyes grew serious. On the other side of the river was Fredericksburg, where 78,000 Confederate soldiers waited. What were the Union soldiers going to do?

And then, as if in answer to her question, she saw a group of Union soldiers running to the river, holding timbers and planks.

"What are they doing?" George wondered aloud.

"They're building a bridge across the water so our soldiers can cross to the other side," Clara said excitedly. But that very moment shots rang out from the Confederate side.

"The Confederate soldiers are shooting hard!" Clara said then. "They won't let them build the bridge.

"Look, George, more Union soldiers are coming. They're putting the planks together. We'll have a bridge after all!" More shots rang out and Clara could see soldiers fall. "Come, George," she said, turning away from the window. "We better start working. I have a feeling we're going to be really busy the next few days."

Sure enough, they had hardly gone downstairs when soldiers brought in the first wounded men. Clara sprang into action. She started big fires in the fireplaces to keep the house warm, and heated some water, which she poured into a basin she brought along as she bent over the soldiers, tending to their wounds.

But that was just the beginning. Clara's intu-

Clara Could See Soldiers Fall.

ition was right. All day the wounded soldiers poured into Lacy House, Clara Barton's battle hospital. Even as she took care of the wounded, Clara could hear the loud cannon fire and the shooting that never stopped.

There was hardly time to think. She kept the fires going and made hot soup. She knew that it was very important to keep wounded soldiers warm, and that was no easy matter in the middle of this harsh winter. Her own fingers were red with the cold, but that didn't stop Clara Barton.

By the middle of the second day even George was a little worried. "Are we going to have enough room here for all the wounded?" he asked Clara as he unrolled bandages.

"We'll *make* room," Clara declared. "We won't turn away anybody."

Suddenly the front door opened and a soldier rushed in, looking all around him. When he saw

Clara, he hurried over to her. "Are you Clara Barton?" he asked her.

"I am."

"This is for you, Miss Barton," he said, handing over a paper note that was crumpled and bloody. Clara read it quickly.

"Who is it from?" George asked her.

"It's from Dr. Clarence Cutter," Clara told him. "He's working on the other side of the river. Our soldiers managed to cross the bridge and are fighting at Fredericksburg."

"What does he want?"

"He says, 'Come to me. Your place is here.'" She looked up at George. "He wants me to go to the other side of the river because there are so many wounded soldiers and no one to nurse them there."

"The other side of the river? Across that bridge?" George's eyes widened. "Don't do that, Miss Barton. The Confederate soldiers are shooting at

The Most Dangerous Thing She'd Ever Done

anyone who crosses the bridge."

But Clara had already put the note into her pocket and taken off her apron. "I must go. Our soldiers are fighting on the other side with no one to take care of them. The other nurses can continue my work here. I must go where I'm needed."

"If you're going," George said, "I'm going, too."

They packed some supplies as quickly as possible and left the Lacy House. At the river Clara stopped, looking across. The wooden bridge lay right on the water, swaying in the freezing winds. Shots rang out from the other shore and sprayed the water on both sides.

Deep inside, Clara knew this was probably the most dangerous thing she'd ever done. Then she put one foot on the bridge. It swayed dangerously from side to side, right over the deep water. Shots rang out again, and she could hear the bullets hitting the water all around her. Clara was afraid. But she thought of the Union soldiers who'd built this bridge. *Some of them even died,* she thought to herself. *The least I can do is cross the bridge they built for me.*

Soon Clara was walking across the bridge, taking one step after another, slowly and calmly, while the bridge swayed from side to side under her feet, wind howled, and bullets sprayed the water all around her. George followed bravely right behind her.

When she approached the opposite shore, a Union officer hurried to help her. He gave her his arm and she grasped it. Just as she stepped down, a cannon shell dropped next to them and exploded. Clara looked down. There was now a big hole in her skirts, and in the officer's uniform.

"This is a warm welcome," Clara said laughingly.

"It is indeed, Miss Barton," the officer said, with

A Big Hole in Her Skirts

admiring glances at the brave woman who'd made the dangerous crossing over the bridge.

Clara worked with Dr. Cutter that entire night and all the entire next day. The Union soldiers were paying a high price for their advance across the bridge. Clara had her arms full every minute, washing wounds, helping Dr. Cutter operate right under the flying bullets, making sure that the soldiers had hot food and enough water. The temperatures were well below freezing and Clara wondered if she would ever get warm again.

Finally she was told to return to Lacy House. When she got back there with George, she couldn't believe her eyes. Every foot of space was covered with wounded. Soldiers were lying on floors, inside corridors and even on stair landings.

"How many wounded soldiers are here?" she asked one of her helpers.

"About 1,200," he told her.

"1,200 men here?" Clara was astounded. "All in this house?"

"What do we do, Miss Barton?" George asked. "Where will we put them all?"

"We must keep the fires going," Clara told him.

"The fires are big," George told her, "but they're not enough. It's freezing."

"We must keep our soldiers warm," said Clara. "I have an idea. Heat up those bricks and wrap them in the soldiers' uniforms."

Just then more soldiers were brought in.

"Wait a minute," George said. The soldiers carrying in the wounded stopped in their tracks. "These wounded soldiers are wearing gray uniforms, not blue. They're Confederate soldiers, not Union soldiers. We can't treat them."

"Why not?" Clara said. "They're risking their lives and getting hurt, too. Of course we'll take care of them."

"Room for Every Soldier."

CLARA BARTON

"But we have no room!" George protested. "We're running out of room even for our own soldiers, never mind enemy soldiers. And you're exhausted and cold. You haven't slept a wink in days and haven't eaten, either."

"They may be enemy soldiers, but they're also wounded men," Clara said. "We have room for all wounded soldiers, no matter what color their uniforms are." She looked around her. "I have an idea. Open up that large cupboard."

George opened it. "There's nothing inside," he said.

"That's the idea," Clara said pleasantly. "Don't you see how large the shelves are? Put some of the wounded soldiers there. And put the others on those sofas over there. We're going to find room for every single soldier who is hurt, no matter what uniform he wears."

For days Clara worked at the Lacy House in

Falmouth, taking care of all soldiers, both Confederate and Union. Her hands were numb with the cold and still she worked on and on, never stopping.

"Have a cup of hot tea," George suggested to her a number of times.

But Clara shook her head. "Time is crucial," she explained. "The quicker the men get treatment for their wounds, the higher their chances of living. I won't stop until all these men have been taken care of."

Once, as she bent over one wounded Union soldier to give him some hot tea, he gripped her arm. "Miss Barton," he whispered.

Clara patted him gently on the hand. "It's all right. You'll be fine. The doctor says your shoulder is wounded, but you'll recover."

But the soldier held her hand tight. "It's not me, Miss Barton. It's my brother, Jimmy. I'm Henry Butler, but it's about my brother, Jimmy."

"What about your brother?" Clara asked him.

"Have you seen him, Miss Barton?"

Clara stared hard at the pale, weak face. "Was he wounded?"

"I don't know, Miss Barton. He was with the Army of the James that went to fight in Pennsylvania, and he used to write us letters, but we hadn't heard from him for six months. Ma is getting older and she'd like to know what really happened to Jimmy. But we haven't been able to find out anything. I thought maybe you knew, Miss Barton."

"It sounds to me like he's missing," Clara said, thinking out loud.

This wasn't the first story she'd heard of soldiers who were missing in the war. Nobody knew what had happened to them. She looked at the soldier lying on the floor, his eyes looking straight into hers. "Henry," Clara said, "when this war is over, I will look for your brother Jimmy. I can't promise you

"That's All I Ask, Miss Barton."

that I'll find him, but at least I'll find out what happened to him."

Henry Butler smiled and lay back. "That's all I ask, Miss Barton," he said.

Clara straightened her back and stood up. *Even when this war is over, it won't be over. Not for so many families.*

Nor for Clara herself. There would still be so much to be done.

Chapter 11

The Search for Missing Soldiers

Clara worked as a Civil War nurse for two more years. But she never forgot her promise to young Henry Butler. Now she was getting hundreds of letters from brothers, sisters and parents of missing Union soldiers.

"Can you imagine how terrible it is to send your son to fight in the war and then never hear from him again?" she said to her sister Sally in Washington. "He might be a prisoner in the hands of the Confed-

She Was Getting Hundreds of Letters.

erate soldiers. He might be lying wounded in one of our hospitals."

"What if he's dead?" Sally said to Clara.

"Then at least I should find out how he died and where his grave lies. That way his family could visit and bring flowers and say prayers."

"*I?*" Sally said with a little smile. "It sounds to me as if Clara Barton is looking for a new job."

Clara laughed. "You know me so well, Sally!" But Clara's dark eyes turned serious again. "The war will end soon," she said. "When that happens, our soldiers will finally be able to go home. But many soldiers will never go home, like Henry's brother, Jimmy. Their families won't know what happened to them. I would like to find out and let them know."

"That's a big job, Clara," Sally said. "How will you do it?"

Clara thought for a minute. "I think I'll write to

CLARA BARTON

President Lincoln and ask him for his help."

So in February, 1865, Clara wrote to Abraham Lincoln, asking for his permission and help in finding missing Union soldiers.

In March she received his answer, authorizing her, on behalf of the United States government, to find out all information about missing soldiers, including prisoners of war. But the job was enormous. At least 200,000 Union soldiers were not accounted for. Most of them were dead, but their families didn't know where they fell or where they were buried. Clara was determined to find out and let them know.

And then the day Clara Barton had prayed and wished for so fervently finally arrived. On April 9, 1865, Robert E. Lee, the Commander of the Confederate armies, surrendered to General Ulysses S. Grant, Commander of the Union army. The Civil War was over.

The Joy Turned to Grief.

CLARA BARTON

Clara was so happy she didn't know whether to laugh or cry. She'd seen so many young men wounded, she'd seen so many die. No more young men coming to her with bullets in their shoulders or their legs, no more bloody bandages, no more surgeons and hospitals and the cries of dying men. For several days Clara—and all of Washington—was filled with joy and relief.

But only five days later the joy turned to grief.

On April 14, Abraham Lincoln and his wife, Mary, went to Ford's theater in Washington to see a play. Lincoln was tired. The Civil War had drained all his energy and he was exhausted. But that night John Wilkes Booth, an actor, made his way into the balcony theater box, above the stage, where Lincoln sat with his wife. Booth raised his pistol and shot the President. By morning, Abraham Lincoln was dead.

Clara was desolate. Her president was dead!

CLARA BARTON

The following day Clara went to visit her sister.

"Do you know, Sally," she said, her voice almost cracking, "that one of the last letters that President Lincoln ever wrote was the letter in which he asked me to find out what happened to our missing soldiers? I must go on with that job. I would be letting him down if I didn't keep on with my efforts."

"But Clara, how will you manage?" Sally asked her. "President Lincoln is dead and you need more money. You will be looking for 200,000 missing soldiers. You will need to pay your assistants and send out thousands of letters. Where will you get the money?"

"I'm getting some money from Congress," Clara told her.

"That won't be enough."

Clara thought a minute. Then her eyes brightened. "I have an idea. I'll give lectures. People will pay to come and listen to the lectures and we'll use

"I Would Be Letting Him Down."

the money to search for our missing soldiers."

"Lectures! About what?"

"About the Civil War," Clara said excitedly. "I'll talk about my experiences as a nurse on the battlefield. People will want to hear those stories, especially when they know that the money goes to find missing soldiers."

"But you don't like to talk in public," Sally reminded her. "And you'll have to travel all over the country!"

"It's true I don't like to talk in public," Clara said. "But maybe if I do it often enough, I won't be so nervous. And I won't mind traveling across our big country and seeing new places. Washington will always be my home, but it will be nice to travel and see other cities, too."

So Clara started traveling around the country, giving talks and lectures about her work during the Civil War. People everywhere people flocked to hear the Angel of the Battlefield, as she was known by now throughout America. They were curious to see in person the brave nurse who had risked her life over and over again to help Union soldiers.

Imagine their surprise when out would come a short woman, no taller than 5'3", slim and straight, wearing a simple dress and with her black hair combed back. Was this little woman the famous nurse who'd saved thousands of American lives right in the line of cannon and artillery fire?

But as soon as Clara started talking, they knew that she was the one. Even though Clara always had notes with her, she usually spoke from memory, and she spoke so well that her listeners could practically see the battles of Fredericksburg and Chantilly and Antietam right in front of their eyes, and relive those times with Clara Barton.

Clara put the money made from the lectures into her efforts to find the missing soldiers. But her

She Opened Her Mouth. Nothing Came Out.

schedule was very heavy and she was getting weak and ill. In her usual Clara Barton style, she continued working and giving lectures and traveling without stop, until one day she came out onstage in Portland, Maine, opened her mouth to speak and nothing came out. She couldn't say one single word.

"You're exhausted," the doctor told her. "You've worked hard during the Civil War and you're still working hard now, three years later. You must stop all work and rest for three years."

"Three years!" Clara said. But it came out a whisper, for she still couldn't talk.

"Three years," the doctor said. "And I know just where you should spend those years. In Europe!"

"Europe!"

"If you stay here you'll never get any rest," the doctor told Clara. "The people in Europe don't know you. They'll leave you alone and you'll be able to get your strength back."

CLARA BARTON

Clara had no choice. She was exhausted and ill. She found other people to continue her work, packed her bags and took a boat across the Atlantic Ocean to Europe in 1869.

But the doctor was wrong. The people in Europe had already heard about Clara Barton. They were waiting for her—and they already had a job for her to do!

Across the Atlantic

Chapter 12

The International Red Cross

"What a beautiful lake!" Clara sighed happily. "And what a beautiful city!"

Madame Golay laughed delightedly. She was taking Clara out for a carriage ride along the lake in Geneva, Switzerland. The Golays were friends of Clara's, and they were only too happy when she chose to stay at their home in Geneva.

Geneva is a beautiful city. It curls around a crystal-clear lake, nestled at the foot of the Alps. The mountain air is clean and crisp—perfect then for a woman who had come to Switzerland in 1869, ill and exhausted.

She turned to her friend. "You've taken such good care of me, Madame Golay. I am so grateful!"

Madame Golay gave Clara a big kiss. "Not as good as the care you gave to our son Jules," she said. "When you found Jules wounded in an American hospital after fighting for the Union, so sick he couldn't even write to us, you helped him write letters so we'd know what happened to him. And you took care of him until he got well. We will never forget that. And now, my dear, I see you are looking a little tired. I think our tour of Geneva has taken long enough. It's time to go home."

On their way home Clara pointed at something. "Look, Madame Golay. That looks like your country's flag, but it's a little different."

Madame laughed. "You're right. The Swiss flag is a white cross on red, and this one is a red cross

"The Flag of the International Red Cross"

on white. That is the flag of the International Red Cross."

"The International Red Cross!" Clara exclaimed. "What's that?"

"I'll explain when we get home," Madame Golay told her.

But when they got home Clara was told that she had visitors waiting for her in the garden. Puzzled, she went out. Two very distinguished-looking gentlemen took their hats off and rose to their feet as she approached.

"Clara Barton?" asked a tall man. "I am Dr. Louis Appia."

"And I," said the second gentleman, "am Henri Dunant. We are the founders of the International Red Cross."

"The Red Cross!" exclaimed Clara. "I saw its flag on the way home just now. But I have no idea what the International Red Cross is, and I don't know who you are."

"But we know who *you* are," said Dr. Appia. "You are Clara Barton, the famous American nurse who worked at the front lines during the Civil War. That's why we've come to talk to you."

Clara, still puzzled, sat down.

"Let me explain," said Henri Dunant. "Miss Barton, have you ever heard of the Battle of Solferino?"

Clara shook her head.

"It was a terrible battle among Italian, French and Austrian soldiers which took place in Italy in 1859, one year before your own Civil War. I watched that battle from a nearby hilltop. Miss Barton, many soldiers fell that day. I watched as the wounded lay on the ground, left to die because doctors were unable to treat them."

"That's exactly what happened in the Civil War," Clara said solemnly.

"But We Know Who *You* Are."

CLARA BARTON

"Forty thousand soldiers were either wounded or killed at the Battle of Solferino," Henri Dunant continued. "Most of those who died would be alive today if they had received medical care in time."

"Then this happens all over the world!" Clara exclaimed. "Not just in America."

"It *did* happen all over the world," Dr. Appia said. "But not any more. You see, Miss Barton, as the result of what Henri Dunant saw at Solferino, he came back to Geneva and together we started the International Red Cross. The Red Cross treaty was signed by 31 countries in 1865, right at the end of your Civil War. The countries who signed the treaty agreed that during times of war, their soldiers will not shoot at any nurses or doctors who care for the wounded on the battlefield. They will even cease fire to let the wounded and dying soldiers be carried from the field. Do you realize, Miss Barton, what a difference that can make?"

"Difference!" Clara exclaimed. "Why, this changes everything. How I wish we had had the Red Cross during the Civil War!"

"The flag with the red cross on white is the flag of the International Red Cross. Soldiers are not allowed to shoot at any doctors or nurses who work under that flag. That is *our* uniform, Miss Barton, and as long as we wear it we can heal the sick and take care of the wounded without fearing for our lives."

Clara clapped her hands together. She felt just like a young girl. "That's the most exciting thing I've ever heard!"

"If that's the case," Henri Dunant said, "then I'd like to ask you one thing, Miss Barton. Why hasn't America signed the Red Cross treaty?"

Clara looked at him in surprise.

He nodded and went on. "Since 1864, we have been asking the United States to participate in the

"To Tell You About the Red Cross."

CLARA BARTON

International Red Cross and sign the treaty, but so far they have refused."

"That's why we came here today," Dr. Appia added. "You see, Miss Barton, you are not just famous in America, you are also famous here, in Europe. Everybody has heard of your heroic efforts on behalf of your soldiers during the Civil War. When we heard that you were staying in our city, we wanted to visit you—tell you about the Red Cross, and ask for your help to convince your country to become a part of it, too. We were sure that you, who have seen so much suffering, would appreciate what the Red Cross does and what it can do in your country, too."

They rose to their feet. Clara rose, too.

"Gentlemen," she said, "I thank you for your visit. You made the right choice in coming to speak to me. Right now I must stay in Europe for a few more years. But I give you my word that when I return to America I will do all I can to convince my government to sign the Red Cross treaty."

Both men bowed. "We could hope for nothing more," Henri Dunant said. "We know that when Clara Barton makes a promise, she keeps it."

They picked up their hats and Clara walked them to the door.

But that night Clara couldn't sleep. Lying in her bed, she kept on thinking of what the two men had told her. Of course, the Red Cross was a wonderful thing. What a difference it would have made to the United States if they had had a Red Cross during the Civil War! What a difference to her work if the shooting would have stopped so that she and other nurses and doctors could have gone onto the battlefield to take care of the wounded! Clara promised herself that, whatever happened, she would go home and convince America to become part of the Red Cross.

That Night, Clara Couldn't Sleep.

CLARA BARTON

A few months later a new war broke out, not in America, but in Europe. Just as in America, Clara Barton was there to take care of the wounded and the dying—with one big difference. This time she did it under the flag of the Red Cross.

Chapter 13

Fighting Again

"Clara! Clara!" Someone was knocking urgently at the door. Clara could hear Antoinette's excited voice.

"What is it, Antoinette?" Clara asked, opening her door.

Antoinette, a young Swiss woman who was now Clara's friend and companion, was very excited. "There is a very elegant woman downstairs to see you," she whispered, her eyes sparkling with excitement. "A grand duchess!"

The Grand Duchess Shook It Warmly.

CLARA BARTON

"A grand duchess! To see me!"

Clara hurried downstairs. Two servants in gold and red uniforms stood at attention as she entered, and a beautiful woman wearing a long gown, with jewelry around her neck and arms, got up from her seat.

"Are you Clara Barton?" she asked in a soft, dignified voice. Clara nodded. "I am Louise, Grand Duchess of Baden and the daughter of King Wilhelm of Germany."

Clara stretched out her hand and the Grand Duchess shook it warmly. Then the two women sat down.

"You must wonder why I've come to visit you, Miss Barton," the beautiful woman said. "I will explain. As you know, war has been declared between Germany and France. German soldiers have advanced into France and are conquering towns and cities on their way to Paris."

Clara nodded. She knew all about it. The fighting was not far from Switzerland, where she was still visiting.

The Duchess continued. "Then you know of the terrible suffering caused by this war, not just for the soldiers but also for the people of France. There is not enough food. Disease and starvation are everywhere. Fires have burned homes, so families have no place to live. Children are walking on the streets, lonely and hungry."

"What can I do?" Clara asked.

The Duchess put her hand out. "Help us, Miss Barton," she said. "We are working with the Red Cross to bring supplies, medical help and food. Come with us. You are very famous for the work you did in the American Civil War. Right now we need you here, in Europe."

Clara thought hard. Her doctor had told her to stop working for three years, and though she had

"Help Us, Miss Barton."

had a good rest for almost a year, she knew she wasn't completely well. But people were sick and dying once again.

She made up her mind fast. "I'll help," she told the Grand Duchess. "Where should we go?"

"To Strasbourg," the Grand Duchess said. "It is a French city which the German soldiers have surrounded. The population has no food or water. The city will fall soon and the people will need help."

"Then we must bring medical supplies and food and water and — "

The Grand Duchess smiled. "You don't have to bring anything, Clara. The Red Cross has taken care of everything. You'll see."

The next day the two women were on their way. As they left Switzerland, the roads filled with refugees—families on foot, all their belongings packed tightly on carts, walking alongside their sheep and cows, all fleeing the city of Strasbourg.

As Clara and the Grand Duchess got closer, they could see the German soldiers who had surrounded the city. What would they do if the soldiers didn't let them through? Clara had an idea. She removed the red ribbon she wore around her neck, quickly made it into a cross and sewed it onto her sleeve. Just as she finished doing that, a German sentry halted their carriage.

"Halt! You cannot proceed any farther."

"But we are nurses!" Antoinette said. "We are going to Strasbourg to help take care of the wounded."

"No one crosses this line!" the German soldier said, holding up his bayonet, the sharp, pointed spear attached to his rifle. "You must turn around."

"We are *Red Cross* nurses," Clara Barton said. "Do you see this?" she pointed to the red cross on her sleeve, the one she had just sewn. "Your country signed a treaty that gives safe passage to Red Cross

"You Must Let Us Through!"

nurses. You must let us through!"

The soldier lowered his bayonet, stepped aside and raised his hat, respectfully. "You are free to go on to Strasbourg. God bless you and your work!"

Clara Barton looked down at the red ribbon on her sleeve. That was the power of the Red Cross. *People respect it everywhere we go!* she thought.

Quickly Clara Barton was to find out even more about the power of the Red Cross. Like all the other big European cities, Strasbourg had a local Red Cross chapter that had stored up medical supplies, linens and food. When the city fell to the German soldiers, the Red Cross sprang into action and distributed its supplies to the population. In addition, other Red Cross cities in Europe began to send urgently needed supplies to the people of Strasbourg.

We had nothing like this during the Civil War, Clara said to herself over and over as she supervised the distribution of the Red Cross supplies and helped take care of wounded soldiers. She did just what she'd done during the battles of Chantilly and Fredericksburg, preparing bandages, feeding soldiers hot soup, making sure they were clean and comfortable and getting medical treatment immediately.

But Fredericksburg had had no storehouses like Strasbourg did now—full of boxes, packages and barrels of food. And there had been no trains in Chantilly to bring emergency supplies from all over Europe, with trained nurses waiting for the food at the stations, the Red Cross emblem sewn on their sleeves.

What a difference this would have made to our soldiers in America, Clara thought. *So many more of them would have lived if we had had all these supplies and trained nurses to help. When I go back home, I must persuade our government to be-*

Storehouse Full of Packages and Food

come part of the International Red Cross. It will be the most important task in my life. But in the meantime there was a lot of work to do right there, in Strasbourg, tending the wounded soldiers.

But Clara's friend Louise, the Grand Duchess, soon talked to Clara about another, even bigger problem. "The people in Strasbourg are suffering very badly, Clara. More than 20,000 of them are without food, clothing or shelter. They are proud people, Clara. The women especially don't wish to receive charity. What shall we do?"

"Aren't there any jobs for them?" Clara asked. "That way they could make money to buy food for their children and they won't need charity."

"But my dear, there are no jobs for anybody," the Grand Duchess said.

"We'll *create* jobs," Clara said. "My mother always told me that all women know how to sew. I will set up a clothing factory where women can sew clothes. The people in Strasbourg need clothing, but there isn't enough right now. If these women sew the clothing, they can sell it for money. With the money they make they will be able to buy the things they need for their families."

So Clara set up a workroom in Strasbourg. The first one was in the yard of a ruined house, but soon it was so successful, Clara opened many such workrooms throughout the city. She bought the materials. The women, working with needles, thread and scissors, turned out dresses, skirts and pants, all of which were sold to the people of Strasbourg.

Three hundred women toiled in the workrooms. With the money they received for the clothes, the women bought food for their families. They didn't need to look for charity because they had jobs— thanks to Clara.

"You are a genius," the Grand Duchess told Clara Barton. By then they had worked together

Clara Finally Packed Her Bags.

with the Red Cross for months and become good friends. "You have given the women of Strasbourg not just clothes and food, but something much more important—their self-respect," the Grand Duchess said.

"They earned it," Clara told her. "They work hard."

"But you worked even harder."

"It wasn't just me," Clara said. "It was the Red Cross. It's the most wonderful organization in the entire world. It must come to America, too. For that reason I must return home.

"I promised Dr. Appia that I will convince our government to sign the treaty and become part of the Red Cross. I won't live in peace until I have succeeded."

So on Christmas Eve, Clara finally packed her bags to go back home. It was cold in the house, and suddenly Clara missed her family. Tomorrow,

CLARA BARTON

Christmas Day, was her birthday. Usually it was full of friends and family, but this year she was celebrating it all alone.

There was a knock on the door. Antoinette went to open it, then called to Clara.

"Clara, come quick!"

Clara hurried to the door. Outside was a large crowd of people—men, women and children. They had come to wish her a Merry Christmas and to say good-bye. In front of them was a big Christmas tree, the biggest she'd ever seen, full of lights like stars and surrounded by flowers and gifts. When the people saw Clara at the door they applauded with shouts of: "God bless you, Miss Barton!" and "We love you, Miss Barton!"

Clara was so overwhelmed, she sat down on the house steps. There was snow on the ground and on the surrounding trees, but she didn't care. Tears came to her eyes even as she smiled.

A Large Crowd of People

CLARA BARTON

One little girl, wearing a beautiful dress that had been made by one of the women who sewed in Clara's workrooms, stepped forward and said, "This Christmas tree is a gift from the people of Strasbourg to Clara Barton. We thank you and love you for all that you have done for us."

Clara held out her hands and kissed the little girl.

"This is the most beautiful Christmas I've ever had," she told them all. "I will never forget you."

Chapter 14

The American Red Cross

Clara Barton leaned back in the elegant wing chair on which she was sitting. She was in the White House in Washington, D.C., waiting to see the President of the United States.

Clara shut her eyes for a few minutes. It was 1878. Finally she was back in Washington. Finally she was back home.

She was tired and would have liked to rest, but she could not forget her promise to Dr. Appia. Even now there was a letter in her pocket from Gustave

President Hayes Entered the Room.

Moynier, President of the International Red Cross, to be delivered to Rutherford B. Hayes, President of the United States. Could she do the job? Could she convince the President to sign the Red Cross treaty so that America would finally join the International Red Cross? It had taken her several years just to get this far, to be able to see the President. Would he listen to her?

She heard footsteps and got up. President Hayes entered the room. He extended his hand to her.

"So this is the Angel of the Battlefield of whom I have heard so much," he said with a big smile, shaking her hand. "And now, Miss Barton, I hear that you have become the Angel in Europe, too."

Clara blushed. "Thank you for your kind words, Mr. President. But the truth is there is a greater Angel of the Battlefield than myself, and that is the International Red Cross. I have brought you a letter from its President, Mr. Moynier."

"I will be delighted to read it, Miss Barton. But let me ask you this. Does the Red Cross just help wounded soldiers in time of war?"

"That is what it has done so far, Mr. President," Clara replied.

"We don't have many wars in America," the President said. "Of course, we had the Civil War in which you, Miss Barton, served so bravely. But America is different from Europe. I hope this country shall never fight another war on its own soil. In that case, Miss Barton—what need will we have of the Red Cross?"

"The Red Cross can do more things than help at time of war, Mr. President," Clara said with great spirit. "The Red Cross can also help when natural disasters strike, such as earthquakes, forest fires, hurricanes, tornadoes or floods. Not a year goes by when Kansas is not struck by tornadoes, or the Mis-

"What Need Will We Have?"

sissippi doesn't flood its banks, or hurricanes don't hit our Southern states. Whenever these things happen, help comes slowly, and sometimes not at all. Families are left homeless with no food or shelter, their life savings gone. The Red Cross will help families during times of terrible catastrophe."

"It sounds like a good idea," the President said. "Let me show this to the Secretary of State, and he will be in touch with you."

"Thank you, Mr. President," Clara Barton said.

Clara went back home and waited and waited, but no answer came from the Secretary.

"I can't understand it," she said one afternoon to her friend and supporter, Dr. Julian Hubbell, who had just come over for tea. "Months have passed and I have not heard from anyone in the government." It was a bright spring day and ordinarily Clara would have loved to be outside planting flowers. But today she was sad. "I feel as if I've failed. I promised Dr.

Appia to do all I could to bring the International Red Cross to the United States, and so far I haven't succeeded."

Suddenly she sat up. Her eyes sparkled.

"I can see you have an idea," Dr. Hubbell said, watching her with a smile.

"I have a *wonderful* idea!" Clara exclaimed. "Why not start the Red Cross right now?"

"Because Congress hasn't signed the treaty," Dr. Hubbell reminded her.

"The Congress hasn't signed the treaty to join the *International* Red Cross," Clara said, "but why can't we start an *American* Red Cross?"

A smile came over Julian Hubbell's bearded face. "Indeed," he replied. "Why not?"

"If we start the American Red Cross and start helping people, that will prove to the President and the Congress what a good thing the Red Cross is!"

Clara couldn't wait. Full of excitement, she

Clara Was Elected Its First President.

arranged for a meeting at her home of all the people who believed in the Red Cross and its work. On May 21, 1881, the Association of the American Red Cross was formed and Clara Barton was elected its first president.

But Clara wanted more.

"It's not enough to have one office of the Red Cross here in Washington," she told the people who had gathered in her house. "We must start Red Cross societies and chapters all over the United States. Those local chapters will gather medical supplies and food, just like they do in Europe, so that whenever a disaster strikes, those supplies will be close by and will reach the area as quickly as possible."

Three American chapters of the American Red Cross were formed. They gathered supplies just like Clara directed, and trained volunteers, nurses and doctors.

CLARA BARTON

Disaster came soon afterwards. A terrible forest fire started in eastern Michigan and burned out of control. Strong winds fanned the flames and helped them spread, and soon newspaper headlines read: "Half of Michigan Ablaze!" Homes and farms burned down. Five thousand people were left homeless.

The new American Red Cross sent crates of food and clothing on trains to Michigan. Clara Barton raised money for more supplies. Her friend Julian Hubbell would go along with the Red Cross supplies to Michigan, helping the injured firemen and the people who were left without homes and crops. For the first time in its history, the red-and-white flag of the Red Cross was raised in the United States.

Clara almost cried when she saw the small flag waving in the wind outside the window of the train that departed for Michigan with Red Cross supplies.

"Your dream is coming true!" Julian Hubbell

Disaster Came Soon Afterwards.

shouted as Clara waved to him when the train began to pull out.

"This is only the beginning!" Clara called. "You'll see."

The Michigan fire was the first time Americans saw what the Red Cross could do in times of emergency. Soon more and more cities and towns started Red Cross chapters throughout the country. Clara knew that it was just a matter of time before the President and the Congress would approve it.

Almost ten years had passed since Clara Barton had promised Dr. Appia that she would do everything in her power to get the Red Cross treaty signed by the United States. On March 1, 1882, President Chester Arthur signed the treaty. That meant that the United States not only had its own American Red Cross, but that it was part of the International Red Cross, too.

It had taken her ten years, but Clara Barton

had kept her promise.

In the future, countries might still go to war. There was nothing even Clara Barton could do to change that. But now at least she had the hope that men in battle would not suffer as badly as they had in the past. With the Red Cross, there could be many more Angels of the Battlefield anywhere in the world that war might break out.

And even in times of peace, there were natural disasters that caused so much suffering. Now too, there would be hope for those innocent victims of fire and flood.

"The City Is Afloat, Clara!"

Chapter 15

Floods in Ohio

Two years later, one of the worst flood disasters of all time hit the United States. Both the Ohio and the Mississippi, two of America's greatest rivers, overflowed at the same time.

Clara Barton hurried to Cincinnati, Ohio. She was met at the railroad station by her friend Dr. Julian Hubbell.

"The city is afloat, Clara!" Dr. Hubbell told her as soon as she got off the train. "Half of Cincinnati is underwater."

"Are people getting food?" she asked right away.

"The people in Cincinnati are getting food. What worries me is what will happen to the people down there," he said, pointing south to where the Ohio River met the Mississippi.

"Down there are 400 miles of river that have flooded towns and farms. Nobody is able to get food to those families because they're far apart and the roads are completely flooded. To make things still worse, Clara, a cyclone struck and uprooted entire houses and farms. Many of these people now have no homes at all. What are we going to do?

"We have all these supplies," he added, pointing at the huge boxes and crates of food and clothing that Clara had brought with her. "We have everything these people need, but what good is it if these supplies are at the railroad station and the people who need them are stuck hundreds of miles down the river?"

"The People Down There," He Said.

CLARA BARTON

"We must find a way to bring the supplies to them," Clara said. "Take me down to the river. I think I have an idea."

The two of them made their way down to the Ohio River. They didn't have far to go. Water had flooded much of Cincinnati. Everywhere Clara looked the water had risen up to the second and even third floors of houses, sometimes covering them completely. Clara looked down to where the river flowed south. No land was to be seen—no banks, no hills, no farms, no dry land. Just water.

"We'll charter a boat," Clara said. "We'll fill it up with supplies and start down the river."

At four o'clock the next afternoon the *Josh V. Throop*, filled to the brim with coal, food and clothing, rang its bell and started down the Ohio River. It flew two flags instead of one. One was the flag of the United States. The other was the flag of the Red Cross. The *Josh V. Throop* was the first Red Cross relief boat ever seen in America.

"What's my destination, Miss Barton?" asked the captain of the *Josh V. Throop*.

"Set course for the first village on the river, captain," said Clara as she stood on the deck, looking at the high waters. "There," she pointed. "I see a group of people standing on a hill on the Kentucky side of the river."

The captain set course and soon moored the *Josh V. Throop* alongside the hill. A sad group of people came down toward the boat. One man, his eyes black with despair and suffering, stepped forward. "Who are you?" he asked Clara, who'd been the first to get off the boat.

"We've come to help you. We're the American Red Cross."

"We're all that's left from the town of Pierpont, Kentucky," the man said. "I'm John Cove, the town's minister. These families all lost their homes and

The Men Began Unloading.

farms. We've had nothing to eat for three days and no way to stay warm. Some of the cattle and the cows have already starved to death and the rest will die within two days."

Clara quickly got to work. At her direction, the men on board the boat began unloading boxes of clothing, food and coal. "Here's enough food and fuel to keep you going for another two weeks," Clara said.

John Cove looked at the supplies on the ground and then at the small woman at his side with amazement.

"In addition," Clara said as more large boxes were brought ashore, "here is food for your animals. When the water goes down, you'll be able to return to your farms, so we've brought corn, oats and hay. And now we must go to the next town," she said with a wave, hurrying back to the *Josh V. Throop*, "but we'll be back in two weeks!"

John Cove hardly had time to say thank you and good-bye before the *Josh V. Throop* was off again, crossing the river.

Julian Hubbell laughed. "I think John Cove thinks he's just seen an angel from God. You appeared out of thin air, bringing all the things these people need—and then you just disappeared!"

Clara smiled, but she knew there were thousands of people down the river, people who had lost everything and were now close to death. "Let's hurry down to the next town, this time on the Illinois side of the river," she told the captain. "There's no time to waste."

Hour after hour, day after day, the *Josh V. Throop* made its way down the flooded Ohio River, bringing urgently needed clothes and food for the people who were stranded and homeless. When they reached Cairo, Illinois after a week, the boat reloaded and made its way right back up river

Down the Flooded Ohio

again, bringing more supplies to the people on the river.

Finally after a few weeks, the waters of the Ohio River began to come down.

"This is good news," the captain told Clara as they made their last delivery to a group of people who were waving good-bye and shouting "hurrah" after the boat. "All these people will now be able to return to their homes and farms. Your work is finished, Miss Barton."

But Clara shook her head. "Not yet, Captain. You see, these people have very little to return to. Their houses were flooded and damaged beyond repair. Even when the waters go down they'll still have no place to live for a long time."

Suddenly, a bright light shone in her eyes.

"Are you getting another one of your ideas?" Julian Hubbell teased her.

"Yes, and this is the best of all!" Clara

exclaimed. "When do we reach Cincinnati again, Captain?"

"Tomorrow morning, Miss Barton."

"Then, Captain, as soon as we arrive, I want you to load this ship with lumber, doors and windows, tools, utensils and groceries. I also want you to take on board a group of carpenters."

"Carpenters?" the captain asked. "Why carpenters?"

"Because we're going to build these people homes," Clara said happily.

The next day the *Josh V. Throop* sailed up to Cincinnati and loaded all the items Clara had asked for, including a group of skilled carpenters. The following day the boat was back on the river. Clara was on deck when she spotted a woman surrounded by children on a desolate shore. Quickly, she told the captain to land and went out to meet the woman.

"I'm Mrs. Plew," the woman told Clara. She was

"These Are My Children."

tall and thin. Her clothes were in tatters. "These are my children." Her children, too, looked thin, with large dark eyes that hadn't seen food in several days.

"Where is your husband, Mrs. Plew?" asked Clara.

"My husband was a river pilot. He died in a flood a few years ago," Mrs. Plew said. "I have six children, from three to fifteen. We had a few horses and cows and chickens, but when the floods came we lost the horses and the cows. Our house was destroyed in a storm."

Clara's heart ached for this woman. "Would you like us to take you and your children on our boat and bring you to Cincinnati?" she asked.

Mrs. Plew looked around her. Her eyes were soft and gentle. "I don't want to leave this place," she finally said, raising herself till she stood up even taller. "I grew up in Indiana, but my husband lived and died here. He's buried here, too, and I don't wish to leave his grave, Miss Barton."

"You are a brave woman," Clara said. "If you wish to stay here, we'll help you."

Immediately the carpenters got to work. Bringing building materials with them, along with their hammers and nails, they began to put up a small, one-room house. At the same time, other Red Cross volunteers brought beds, clothing, tables and chairs, dishes, a small stove, candles, farming tools and cooking utensils from the boat. Last of all, they brought out a big supply of meat, cornmeal and groceries.

In three hours the work was done. Mrs. Plew looked with astonishment at the new clean house and the warm fire blazing in the hearth. Her daughter had begun to cook dinner for the younger children who were seated around the fire, getting warm for the first time in weeks.

In Three Hours, the Work Was Done.

"And here is $100.00 for you," Clara said. "Thousands of people throughout this country have sent money to be given out to the survivors of the floods. You are a courageous woman. I'm sure you'll be able to use this money to help start a new life for yourself and your children."

Mrs. Plew looked with wonder at the money in her hand and the house in which she now stood. "I can hardly believe this," she said. "This morning I thought we'd lost everything and the end was near. Now suddenly we have a house and some money to begin again." She looked at Clara. "Who are you? Why do you do this?"

"Our job is to help people like you," Clara told her.

Mrs. Plew looked at the white and red flag on the *Josh V. Throop*. "What flag is that?" she asked.

"That is the flag of the Red Cross," Clara told her. "And the people you see here are Red Cross volunteers who help people in bad times like these. And the food and lumber and furniture comes from donations that people have sent in to the Red Cross to help people like you. You are not alone, Mrs. Plew. Thousands of people across this country care about you and your family."

Tears shone in the woman's face. "God bless you," Mrs. Plew said, giving Clara Barton a big hug. "And God bless the Red Cross."

"I've Brought More Company."

Chapter 16

Glen Echo

"Come in, Stephen, come in." Clara Barton greeted her nephew at the door. "Come see my new house."

"Aunt Clara, I've brought more company," Stephen said.

Clara clapped her hands happily. "You know how much I love company, Stephen. Please introduce me to my young guests."

Stephen walked in, accompanied by two children. "This is Mary and Billy, the children of my friends, the Delaneys. When they heard I was coming to visit my favorite aunt they begged me to take them along."

"We wanted to meet you, Miss Barton," Billy said. "You're so famous—everybody knows who you are!"

"Why, thank you, Billy," Clara said. "I am always happy when children come to visit me."

"So this is your new house," Stephen said, looking around him. "Aunt Clara, this is as big as a warehouse!"

"It has thirty-eight rooms and thirty-six closets!" Clara said. She smiled as Billy and Mary walked from one room to another, their eyes getting bigger and bigger. "That way I have plenty of room for Red Cross supplies for emergencies."

"What kind of supplies, Miss Barton?" Mary asked.

"Oh, you know, first-aid kits, linens, lots of ban-

"We Wanted to Meet You."

dages, lots of canned food and blankets. All the things that people need in time of an emergency."

Stephen laughed. "Aunt Clara is always thinking about the Red Cross and what it will need!"

"As a matter of fact," Clara said with a twinkle in her eye, "guess what the name of the house is."

"*Red Cross!*" Billy said.

"You guessed right!" Clara Barton said. "Red Cross at Glen Echo, Maryland."

"I should have known," Stephen said, shaking his head and laughing.

Clara took her nephew, along with Billy and Mary, to the sitting room at the south of the house. Through the windows they could see the Potomac River. Clara brought out iced tea and cookies. "I baked these fresh today," Clara said. "Have some."

"This is a big house," Billy said. "Do you have many servants, Miss Barton?"

Clara laughed. "No, Billy. As a matter of fact, I

take care of this house all alone. You know what I did last night? I folded all the sheets and linens and clothes that had been washed. This morning I started ironing at six and continued till it was finished, at one in the afternoon! And just before you came I baked these cookies. I had a feeling I might have some young guests."

"My goodness, Aunt Clara," Stephen said admiringly, "don't you ever stop working?"

"Never!" Clara said. "I do my own gardening and cooking. And do you know how many hundreds of letters I receive every day, especially from young people all over this country? I answer every single one."

"Miss Barton," Mary said, looking up bashfully at Clara. "I want to become a Red Cross nurse, just like you. I want to take care of wounded soldiers like you did in the Civil War."

"And I want to be a Red Cross volunteer," Billy

"That's a Fine Thing to Want," Clara Beamed.

said, looking proudly at Clara. "I want to go with the Red Cross whenever something terrible happens, like a flood or a hurricane or a bad fire. I want to give out clothes and food, too, and help people build homes, just like you do."

"That's a fine thing to want," Clara said, beaming at both Billy and Mary. "But working with the Red Cross doesn't just mean traveling to distant places. In fact, you can start preparing right now."

"How, Miss Barton?" Mary asked.

"As Red Cross volunteers, there are many things you'll need to know, like how to cook and sew and provide first-aid. We now give first-aid classes, even to children your age."

"Do we really have to learn all those things?" Billy asked.

"When I was your age I learned how to cook and sew, and I took care of little animals when they got sick. I even took care of my older brother David when he fell and got hurt. All those things came in very handy for me when I had to nurse and feed soldiers and sew clothes in Strasbourg. And the wonderful thing is, you don't have to wait till you grow up to learn these things. You can start right now. In a few years you'll be ready to join the Red Cross."

"That sounds like a long time," Billy said.

"Don't worry," Clara said. "Several years will pass very quickly. When you're ready, the Red Cross will be there."

Clara Barton looked down the Potomac River in the direction of Washington, D.C., where she had lived for so many years. "The Red Cross has been here for more than 25 years," she said with a big smile, "and it will be here for just as long as we need it."

Clara Barton died in 1912. But the good she did in caring for the sick, the wounded, and the needy lives on in the hearts of the American people. The

Clara Looked Down the Potomac.

work of the American Red Cross is Clara Barton's living memorial—today and always.

The Red Cross is so much a part of American life today that it's hard to believe that Clara had to work as hard and as long as she did to get it established. And many people have no doubt forgotten the name of the little woman who made it happen.

But every time the Red Cross answers the call of someone in distress, someone victimized by fire or flood or hurricane, the rescuers and volunteers who come to help are there because of the Angel of the Battlefield—a great American woman, Clara Barton.

The Angel of the Battlefield